Tell Me All About You, Mum

A STUDIO PRESS BOOK

First published in the UK in 2025 by Studio Press,
an imprint of Bonnier Books UK,
5th Floor, HYLO, 105 Bunhill Row, London EC1Y 8LZ

www.bonnierbooks.co.uk

Written by Lucy Dowling
Edited by Georgina Kyriacou
Designed by James King
Cover designed by Maddox Philpot
Production by Giulia Capparelli

Text © Studio Press 2025
Illustrations © Shutterstock

All rights reserved. No part of this publication may be reproduced, stored in a retrieval system, or transmitted by any form or by any means, without the prior permission in writing of the publisher, nor be otherwise circulated in any form of binding or cover over than that which it is published and without a similar condition including this condition being imposed on the subsequent purchaser.

A CIP catalogue record for this book is available from the British Library
Printed and bound in Slovakia

1 3 5 7 9 10 8 6 4 2

ISBN: 978-1-83587-405-9

The authorized representative in the EEA is Bonnier Books Uk (Ireland) Limited.
Registered Office address: Floor 3, Block 3, Miesian Plaza
50–58 Baggot Street Lower,
Dublin 2, D02 Y754, Ireland.

compliance@bonnierbooks.ie

Tell Me All About You, Mum

Written by
Lucy Dowling

Draw a picture of yourself here.

Mum, mummy, ma, mother ...

If you have been given this book, it means someone special in your life sees you as their mother figure and wants to know your story. This is not just a book for a biological parent – it's for anyone who has taken on the role of caring for, and guiding, a child.

From the child's point of view, it can be difficult to see the person behind the parent figure, which is where this book comes in. You are a person who has experienced a full life – someone with dreams and ambitions, with life experience and advice worthy of being passed down.

We hope you can use the prompts and questions within the pages of this book to bring your story to life and create a priceless gift for your child that they can treasure forever.

This book was filled out by…

....

for

....

I would like to tell you my story.

Stick a recent photo of yourself here.

Full name: ....
Age when filling this in: ....
Hair colour: ....
Eye colour: ....
Height: ....
Occupation: ....
Relationship status: ....

I started this book on:

....

Location when filling this in:

....

And I am feeling

....

about filling this in for you.

I hope after you finish reading this, you feel:

....

....

....

The one thing I'd like you to take away from my life story is:

....

....

....

....

Date: .... Signed: ....

Tell Me All About Your Childhood

Stick a photo of yourself as a baby here.

Maiden name: ....
Date of birth: ....
Place of birth: ....
Time of birth: ....
Weight at birth: ....
Star Sign: ....
Birthstone: ....
Hair colour: ....
Eye colour: ....

What song was Number One the day you were born?

Do you share your name with anyone special?
....

Did you have any nicknames when you were little?

Did people say that you looked more like your mother or your father?

....

Do you know what your first word was?

....

Did you have a favourite toy as a baby?

....

What was your earliest memory?

....

....

Did you live in a house or a flat when you were a child?

....

If you remember it, write your old address
or street name on the letter above.

Describe your childhood bedroom:

....

....

....

What did you love most about your bedroom or house?

....

....

....

Did you have a garden or outside space to play in?

....

What was the name of the town, city or village that you grew up in?

....

Did you ever have a favourite home?

....

Did you have any secret dens or hiding places?

....

Do you remember your neighbours? What were their names?

....

....

....

Do you remember any neighbourhood traditions?

....

....

Did you attend nursery or did you have a nanny or a childminder?

....

What was the name of your first school?

....

Stick a picture of yourself from your first year of school here.

What did your school uniform look like?

....

....

What were the names of your close friends at primary school?

....

....

What was the name of your first teacher?

....

Draw your school's logo
in the shield.

What was your favourite thing about primary school?

....

And your least favourite thing?

....

What was your favourite game to play in the playground?

....

What did you want to be when you grew up?

....

Share a happy memory of your time at primary school:

....

....

....

Did you collect anything?

....

What were your favourite toys to play with?

....

Did you have any hobbies outside of school?

....

Was there somewhere you loved visiting as a child, such as a park, restaurant, or museum?

....

....

Can you remember three places you visited with your family on holiday? Write them on the postcard.

1. ....

2. ....

3. ....

Did you enjoy playing sports and were you part of a team?

....

....

Did you grow up in a strict
household with rules to follow? ....

....

....

What was the naughtiest thing you did as a child?

....

....

Were you ever scared of anything?

....

Did you grow out of this fear?

....

Who or what made you feel safe as a child?

....

What was your favourite meal when you were young?

....

....

....

Was there a meal that you hated as a child? Do you like it now?

....

Did you have a favourite outfit or piece of clothing?

....

Did you have an imaginary friend? What was their name?

....

How did you celebrate birthdays throughout your childhood?

....

....

What was the best gift you ever received?

....

Was there a toy or book that you always wanted but never received?

....

What was the first music album or single you ever owned?

....

Write the title of your favourite childhood book on the cover.

What were your three favourite movies or TV shows?
1. ....
2. ....
3. ....

Who were your three favourite bands or singers?
1. ....
2. ....
3. ....

Stick some childhood photos of yourself in the frames.

Stick a picture of yourself at secondary school here.

What was the name of your secondary school?

....

Did you have a favourite teacher? What was their name and why were they so special?

....

....

Did you ever get detention at secondary school? What did you do?

....

....

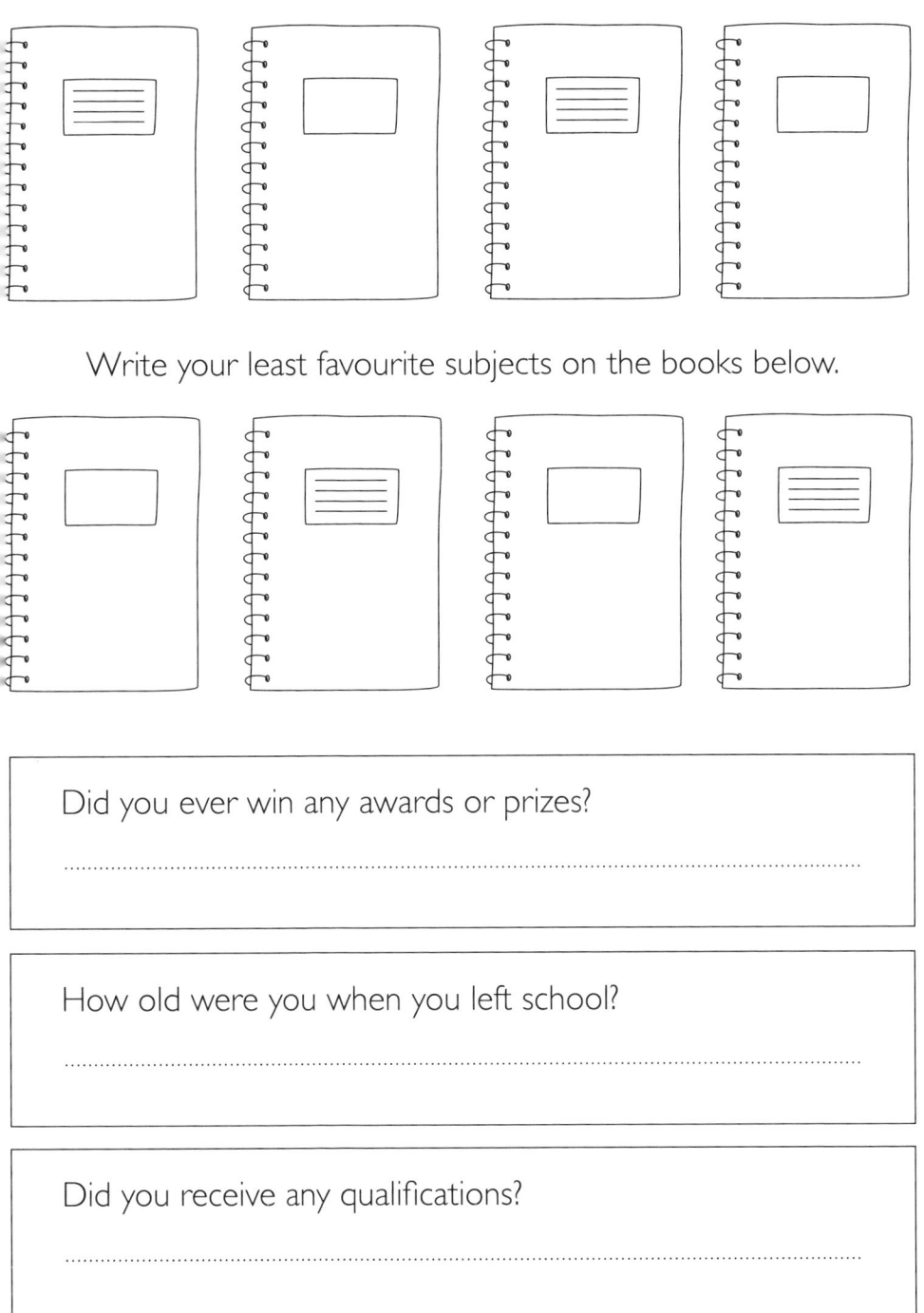

What was your style as a teenager? Did you follow the latest trends?

....

....

What was the craziest fashion trend of the time? How long did it last?

....

....

Where did you buy your clothes from?

....

....

Tell me about your worst fashion faux pas:

....

....

Did you ever get any piercings or tattoos during your teenage years?

....

....

Were you allowed to dye your hair?

....

Did you learn to drive?
If you did, how old were you when you passed your driving test?

DRIVING LICENSE

Age:

....

Date:

....

If not, what was your reason for choosing not to?

....

What music did you listen to when you were a teen?

....

Who was your celebrity crush?

....

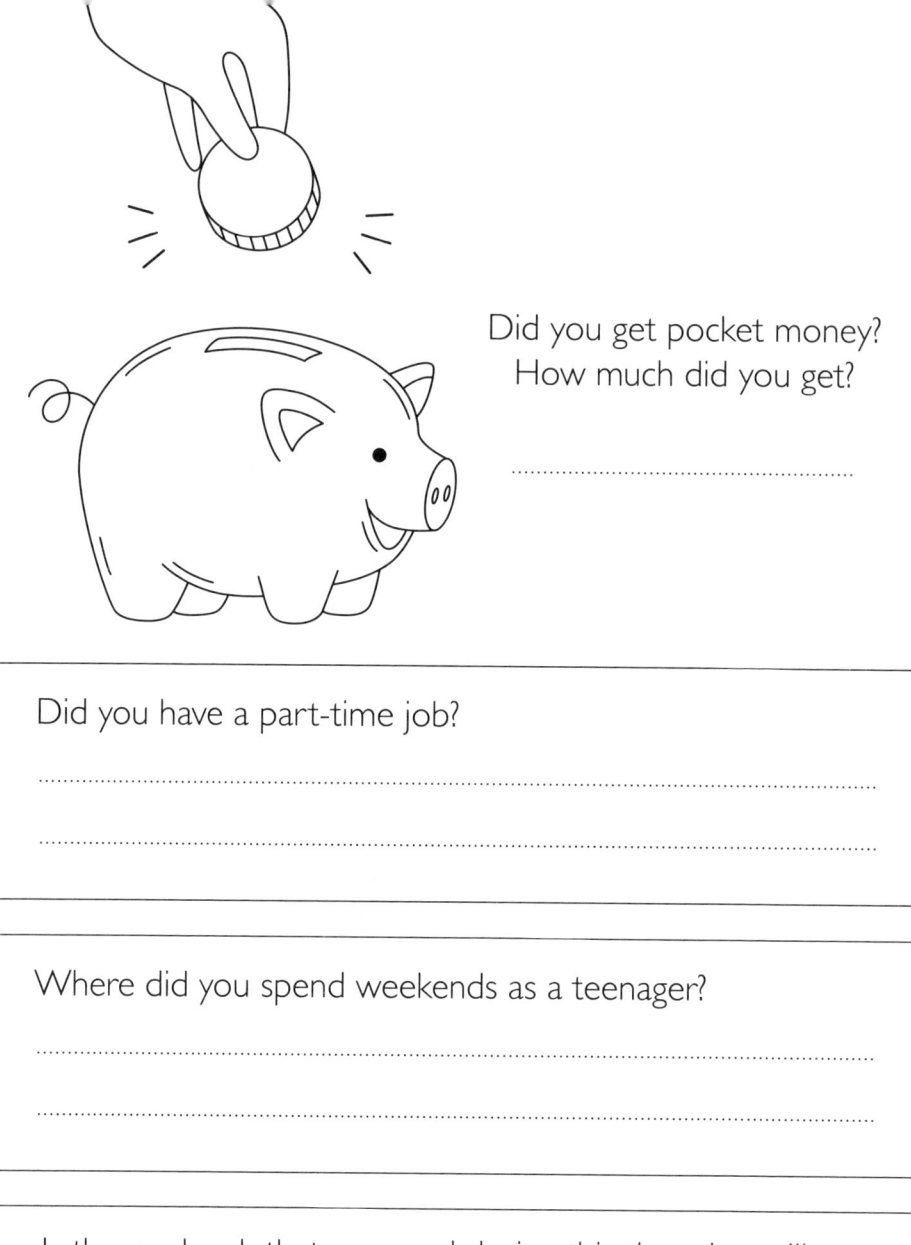

Did you get pocket money?
How much did you get?

....

Did you have a part-time job?

....
....

Where did you spend weekends as a teenager?

....
....

Is there a book that you read during this time that still stands out to you today?

....
....

What was the must-have gadget of the time?

....

Tell me about a holiday you went on with your friends:

....

....

....

Did you ever have a holiday romance?

....

....

Tell me about the time you felt the most confident:

....

....

Write down something you found difficult about being a teenager:

....

....

....

....

Did you always follow the rules or were you rebellious?

....

What was the sneakiest thing you remember doing? Did you get caught?

....

....

What was the biggest lie you ever told as a teenager?

....

....

Who was your first date with?

....

How old were you?

....

Where did you go?

....

How did you celebrate your 18th birthday?

....

....

How did you celebrate your 21st birthday?

....

....

Was there a social cause you were passionate about? Write it on the protest sign.

Tell me about a memory from your teenage years that still makes you smile:

....

....

....

What was your biggest achievement as a teenager?

....

....

....

Tell me about the biggest regret you have from this time:

....

....

....

If you could go back and give your teenage self a piece of advice, what would it be?

....

....

....

....

Is there something you now know that you wish you had known when you were younger?

....

....

....

What was your biggest fear throughout your teenage years and did you overcome it?
....
....
....
....

If you met your teenage self for coffee, what would you tell her?
....
....
....
....
....
....
....
....
....
....
....
....

Stick some photos of yourself as a teenager in the frames.

Tell Me All About Your Journey Through Adulthood

Stick a picture of yourself in your twenties here.

Did you go to college or university after school?

....

If you did, where did you go and what did you study? If not, which path did you choose instead?

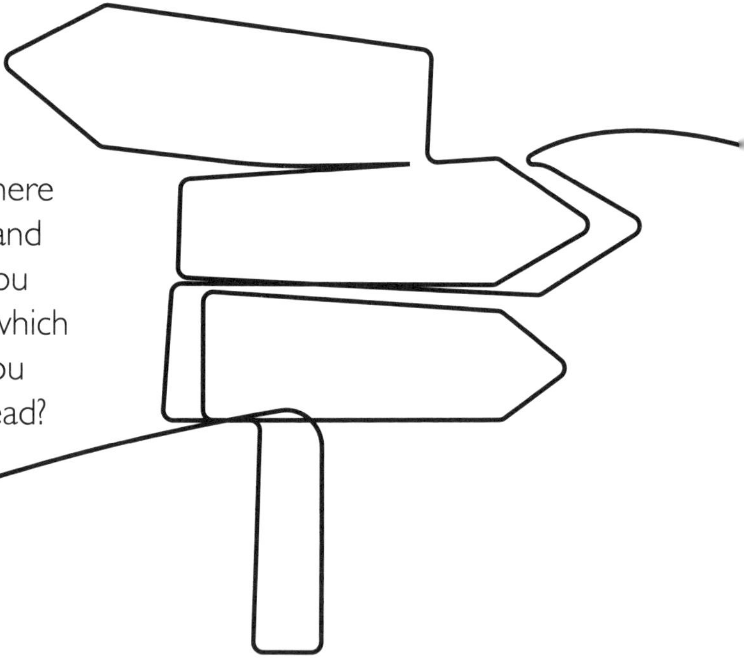

How old were you when you moved out of your childhood home?

....

Did you live in a house or flat and who did you live with?

....

....

Which city or town did you move to?

....

Did you spend any time travelling abroad?

....

....

Tell me about a moment where you felt truly independent and like a true adult:

....

....

....

....

Tell me about your first job:

Occupation: ....

Company: ....

Joined: ....

Departed: ....

What was your salary?

....

Was it a job that you wanted to stay in long-term?

....

....

What was the biggest challenge you faced in your career as you were starting out?

....

....

Tell me about your first achievement at work:

....

....

What is the best job that you ever had?

And the worst?

Tell me about the funniest thing that ever happened at work:

What was your ultimate career ambition as a young adult?

Have you achieved it?

Would you describe yourself as being more of an introvert or an extrovert?
....
....

What did you do to stay healthy?
....
....

Did you have any bad habits?
....
....

Tell me about a special trip or holiday that you went on during this period of your life:
....
....

Did you watch a film that changed your perspective of the world?
....

Describe a party that you will always remember. Fill the disco ball with words to describe the night.

Is there a song that makes you feel nostalgic about this time of your life?

....

What was your biggest achievement ...

... in your 20s:

....

....

....

... in your 30s:

....

....

....

... in your 40s:

....

....

....

Tell me about about a difficult decision that you had to make as an adult:

....

....

Who or what helped you get through hard times?

....

....

If there is one thing you could go back and do differently in your life, what would it be?

....

....

....

....

Is there something that you want me to know about you?

....

....

Share a happy memory that still makes you laugh out loud today:

....

....

Is there a piece of advice you were given during this time that you'll always remember?

....

....

....

....

Where do you live now, and with who?
....
....

If you're working, what is your occupation?
....

What little things bring you joy? Write them in the stars.

☆ ☆ ☆

How do you like to unwind?
....
....

Write three things that you have ticked off your bucket list:
1. ....
2. ....
3. ....

Tell me your biggest worry in life right now:

....

What do you value most in your life?

....

What is the best decision you ever made?

....

....

Fill in each heart with what you love most about yourself.

Are you happy?

....

....

....

Tell me your favourite …
- city: ....
- colour: ....
- animal: ....
- drink: ....
- time of the day: ....
- sandwich: ....
- karaoke song: ....
- song to dance to: ....
- song to cry to: ....
- perfume: ....
- pizza topping: ....

Who would play you in a biopic?

....

Is there a health or beauty product that you just can't live without?

....

What do you always carry in your handbag?

....

Do you have a secret talent?
....
....

Tell me a bad joke:
....
....

What is your most prized possession?
....
....

Do you have any phobias?
....
....

If you were stranded on a desert island what item would you want to be stranded with?
....
....

Look at the options below and tick your preference.

☐ Health or wealth ☐

☐ Follow your heart or follow your head ☐

☐ Dog or cat ☐

☐ Listen or talk ☐

☐ Teach or learn ☐

☐ Take a risk or play it safe ☐

☐ Books or TV ☐

☐ Sunrise or sunset ☐

☐ Beach or mountains ☐

☐ City life or country living ☐

☐ Shower or bath ☐

☐ Sweet or savoury ☐

☐ Ice cream or ice lolly ☐

☐ Tea or coffee ☐

☐ Early riser or night owl ☐

☐ Gold or silver ☐

☐ Fast fashion or timeless pieces ☐

☐ Cosy night in or wild night out ☐

Use a colouring pencil to shade in the countries that you have visited.

What is the best country you have visited and why?
....
....

Are there any places you would still like to visit?
....
....

Stick some photos of yourself as an adult in the frames.

Tell Me All About Your Family and Significant Relationships

Fill in your family tree.

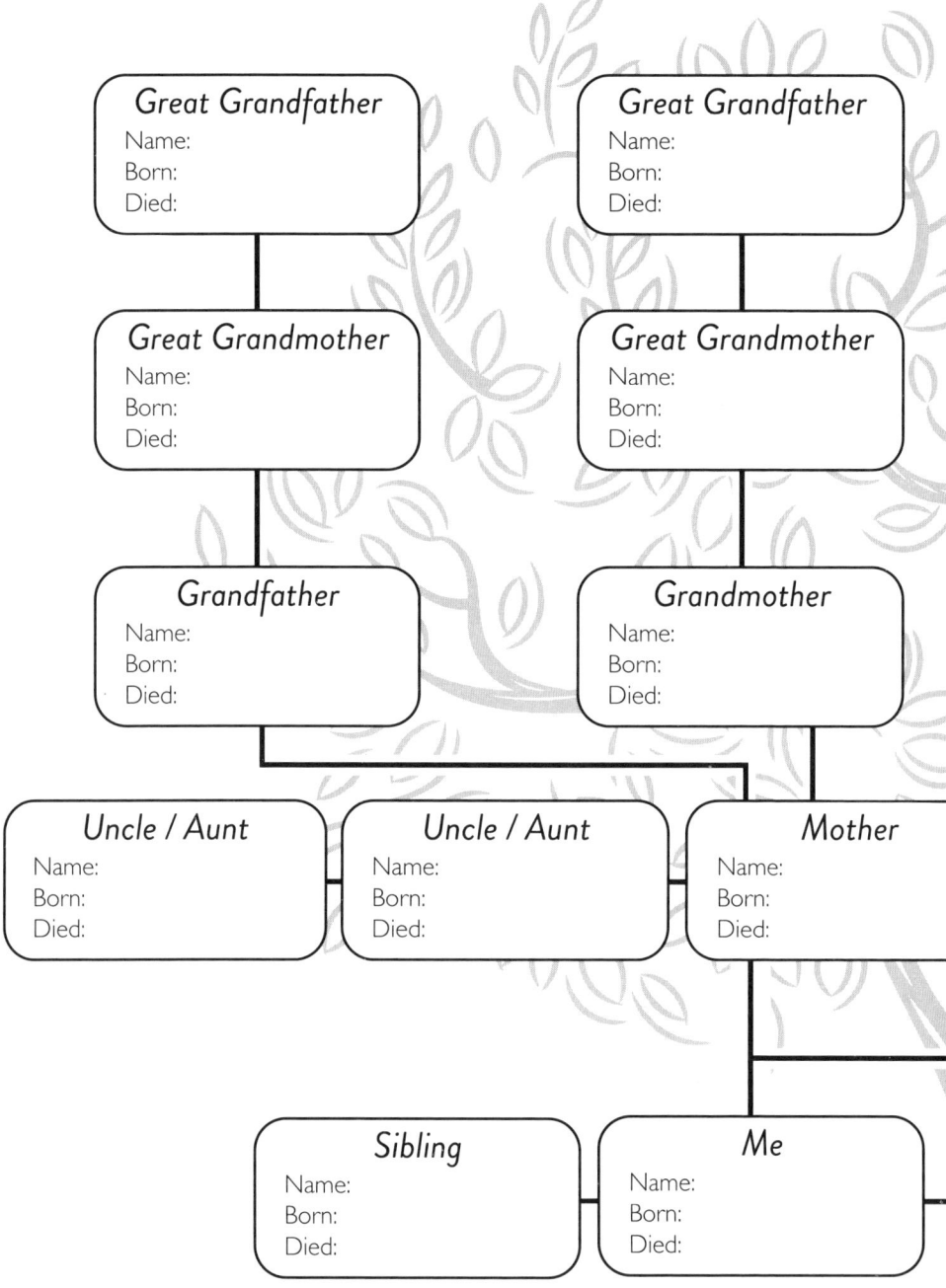

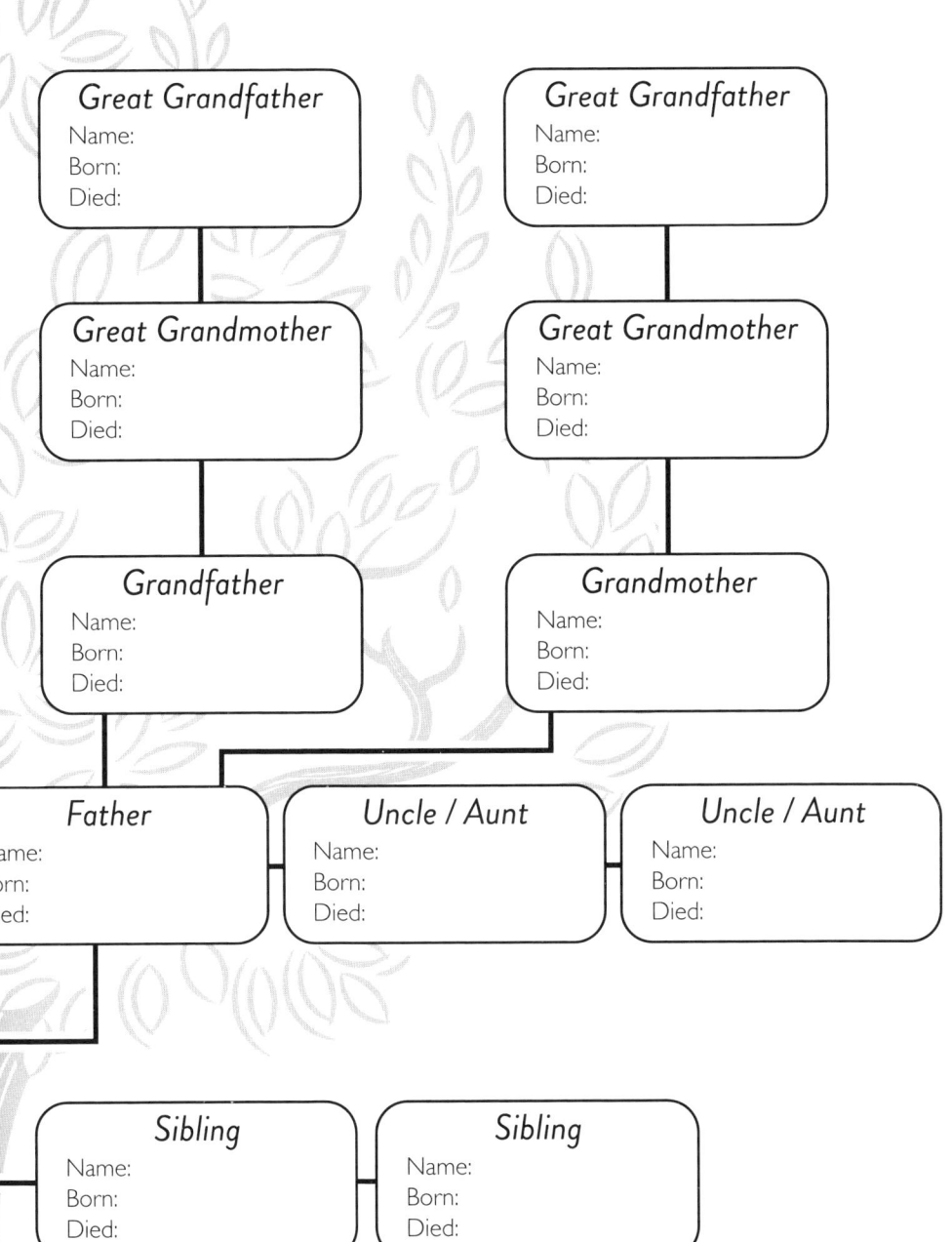

Draw or stick a picture of your mother here.

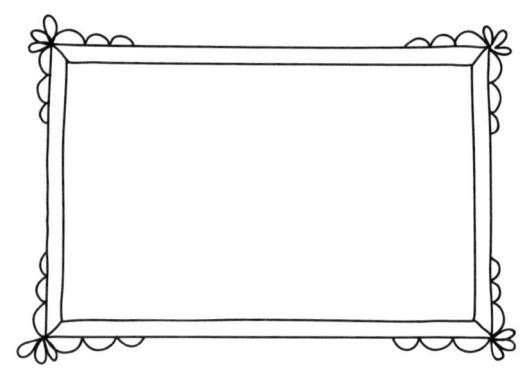

Where was your mother born and where did she grow up?
....

What is the first memory you have of your mother?
....

What smell reminds you of your mother?
....

What similarities do you and your mother share?
....

Tell me the most important life lesson your mother taught you:
....

Draw or stick a picture of your father here.

Where was your father born and where did he grow up?

....

What did you call your father?

....

What is your favourite memory of your father?

....

What similarities do you and your father share?

....

What is the one thing you want everyone to know about your father?

....

Use this space to write about your siblings or, if you prefer, any cousins or friends you consider as family.

First name:	First name: ....
Middle name(s):	Middle name(s): ....
Surname:	Surname: ....
Date of birth:	Date of birth: ....
Place of birth:	Place of birth: ....
Nickname:	Nickname: ....
Eye colour:	Eye colour: ....
Hair colour:	Hair colour: ....

How are you and your sibling(s) similar?

....

....

How do you differ from your sibling(s)?

....

....

What do you love most about them?

....

....

Write a fond memory you have of your sibling(s) in the thought bubble.

Write down an important lesson that they taught you:

....

....

Tell me about a time you did something you shouldn't have, and your sibling(s) got the blame:

....

....

Are you still close to your sibling(s) now?

....

....

....

....

Where was your maternal grandfather born and where did he grow up?

....

How old was he when he met your grandmother?

....

Did you get to meet your maternal grandfather?

....

....

Share a fond memory of him here. If you don't have one, share a story you have been told.

....

....

....

....

Write an incredible fact about your maternal grandfather:

....

....

....

Where was your maternal grandmother born and where did she grow up?

....

Did she have any siblings?

....

Did you get to meet your maternal grandmother?

....

....

Share a fond memory of her here. If you don't have one, share a story you have been told.

....

....

....

....

Is your mother more like her father or mother?

....

....

....

Where was your paternal grandfather born and where did he grow up?

....

Did he have any siblings?

....

Did you get to meet your paternal grandfather?

....

....

Share a fond memory of him here. If you don't have one, share a story you have been told.

....

....

....

....

Is your father more like his mother or his father?

....

....

....

Where was your paternal grandmother born and where did she grow up?

....

How old was she when she met your grandfather?

....

Did you get to meet your paternal grandmother?

....

....

Share a fond memory of her here. If you don't have one, share a story you have been told.

....

....

....

....

Write an incredible fact about your paternal grandmother:

....

....

....

Did your family have any fun traditions?

....

Was there a special place in the family home where you all spent the most time together?

....

Who has the best sense of humour in your family?

....

Write a word that starts with each letter in the word FAMILY to describe what your family meant to you growing up.

F ....

A ....

M ....

I ....

L ....

Y ....

Can anyone in your family speak another language?

....

Did your family practise a religion and attend a place of worship?

....

....

Did you ever celebrate religious festivals or holidays with together?

....

....

What food was central to your family growing up?

....

Did you have any pets? Write their names and breeds below.

Use the space below to write about a significant friendship you've had that shaped who you are today.

Name: ....

Age you met: ....

Where you met: ....

Are you still friends now?

....

Why was this friendship so special?

....

What has this friendship taught you?

....

....

What reminds you of this friend?

....

Who was your primary school best friend and are you still in touch today? ....

....

Who was your best friend at secondary school?

....

Did you ever have a work best friend?

....

Is there a friend that you wish you never lost touch with?

....

Do you have more or less friends now that you're older?

....

Tell me about a time you made amends with a friend who might have let you down:

....

....

....

....

Which of your friends is the most like you?

....

Who is your best friend now?

....

Tell me all about the love of your life:

- Name: ....
- When did you meet? ....
- Where did you meet? ....
- Are you still in touch? ....
- What did this relationship teach you about yourself and love in general?

  ....

- Why was this relationship so significant?

  ....

- How much of your heart did you give away in this relationship? Shade it in the heart opposite.

Did you ever get married?

....

Did you always want to have a family?

....

Tell me about a time you had your heart broken.
How did you heal?

....

....

List the three main things you need to make a relationship work:

1. ....
2. ....
3. ....

If someone does these three things, it's time to walk away from the relationship:

1. ....
2. ....
3. ....

Use the space below to mention another important romantic relationship.

- Name: ....
- Age you met: ....
- Where you met: ....
- Are you still in touch now? ....

Stick some photos of family members, friends and lovers here.

Tell Me All About You and Me!

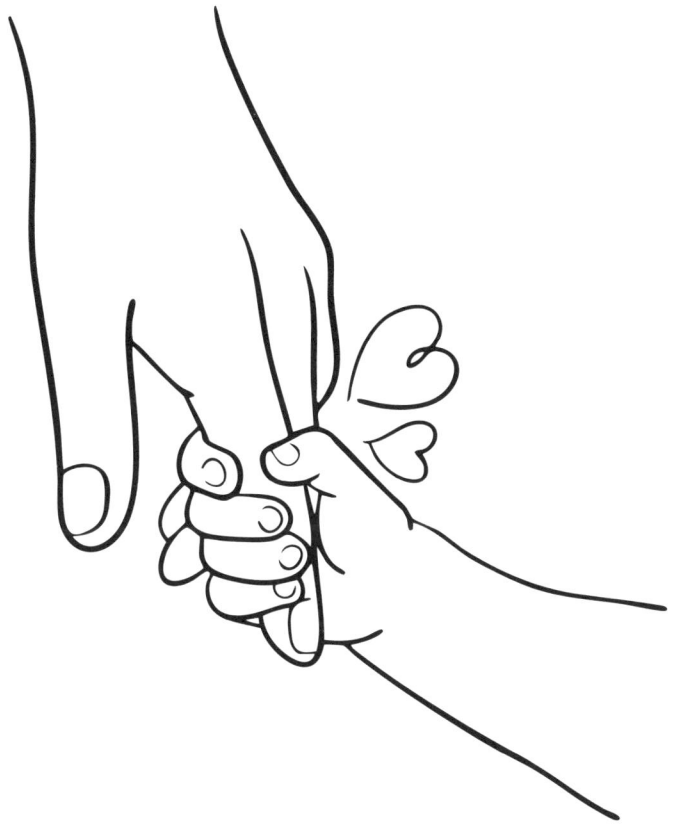

Stick one of the earliest photos of us here.

Fill in the fact file about me below:

- Date of birth: ....
- Place of birth: ....
- Time of birth: ....
- Weight at birth: ....

Who was the first person you told about me?

....

....

How did you feel when you first saw me?
Write the words on a heart in the jar.

Can you remember the first thing I said to you?

....

What is the story behind my name?

....

....

What was my favourite toy or book? Draw it below.

Tell me your favourite thing that we used to do together:

....

....

....

What was the naughtiest thing I ever did as a child?

....

....

....

Did I say any funny words or phrases?

....

....

....

When were you most proud of me as a child?

....

....

....

Do you remember the words to my favourite childhood song?

....

....

....

Share a memory of me that makes you smile:

....

....

....

....

If you could go back to one part of my childhood and relive it, which part would you choose?

....

....

....

What was I like as a teenager?

....

....

What was your favourite way to spend time together?

....

....

Tell me your favourite memory of us from my teenage years:

....

....

What accomplishment were you most proud of me for? Write it in the rosette.

What did you really think of my best friend?

....

....

Did you like my first partner?

....

....

When did I make you the most angry?

....

....

Tell me the one thing you want me to remember about you from when I was a teenager:

....

....

....

What is the hardest thing about being my mother?

....

....

What is one of the best things about being my mother?

....

....

What do you enjoy most about spending time with me now?

....

....

....

Is there something you wish we did more of together?

....

....

Is there anything you wish I understood better about you?

....

....

Tell me about a recent time where you were proud of me:

....

....

If you could give me anything in the world, what would it be?

....

....

....

Is there something you want to tell me, but haven't yet found the words?

....
....
....
....

Is there something you see in me that I might not see in myself?

....
....
....

Is there anything I can do to make our relationship stronger?

....
....
....

What is your biggest hope for my future?

....
....
....

Stick some recent photos
of you and me together in the frames.

What Do You Want Me to Hold On to?

What is your best advice for a happy and healthy life?

....

....

Is there a family tradition you would like me to keep going?

....

....

Are there any family heirlooms you would like me to treasure forever?

....

....

What should I remember when I'm feeling sad or worried?

....

....

....

What is your best advice if I have a child just like me?

....

....

If you had one wish for me, what would it be? Write it in the shooting star.

What song should I listen to when I'm missing you?

....

Share a memory from your family you would like me to hold on to:

....

....

How would you like to be remembered?

....

....

My Hand is Yours to Hold

Use the pages below to draw around your hands as they are now.
Sketch in any lines, scars, tattoos or jewellery.

Left Hand

Right Hand

Use the space below to share a family recipe that you would like to pass down.

Dish

Ingredients

Method

A Letter From You to Me

Use this space to write me a letter. It can be as short
or as long as you like (feel free to add extra pages of paper).
You can use this letter to talk about anything not covered in this
book, or anything that is on your mind or in your heart.
Something for me to hold on to forever.

....
....
....
....
....
....
....
....
....
....
....
....
....
....